CHI

✓

This Is the Way We Go to School

A Book About Children Around the World

This Is the Way We Go to School

A Book About Children Around the World

by EDITH BAER

illustrated by
STEVE BJÖRKMAN

SCHOLASTIC
HARDCOVER

SCHOLASTIC · NEW YORK

No part of this publication may be reproduced in whole or in part, or stored in a retrieval system, or transmitted in any form or by any means, electronic, mechanical, photocopying, recording, or otherwise, without written permission of the publisher. For information regarding permission, write to Scholastic Inc., 730 Broadway, New York, NY 10003.

Copyright © 1990 by Edith Baer.

Illustration copyright © 1990 by Steve Björkman.

Baer, Edith.
    This is the way we go to school / by Edith Baer; illustrated by Steve Björkman.
        p. cm.
    Summary: Describes, in text and illustrations, the many different modes of transportation children all over the world use to get to school.
    ISBN 0-590-43161-7
    1. Vehicles—Pictorial works—Juvenile literature. [1. Vehicles. 2. Transportation.] I. Björkman, Steve, ill. II. Title.
TJ147.B24   1990
629.04–dc20   89-48511
                                               CIP
                                               AC

12 11 10 9 8 7 6 5 4 3 2 1   0 1 2 3 4 5/9

Printed in the U.S.A.   36

First Scholastic printing, September 1990

Designed by Tracy Arnold

One by one or two by two—
Come along, it's fun to do!

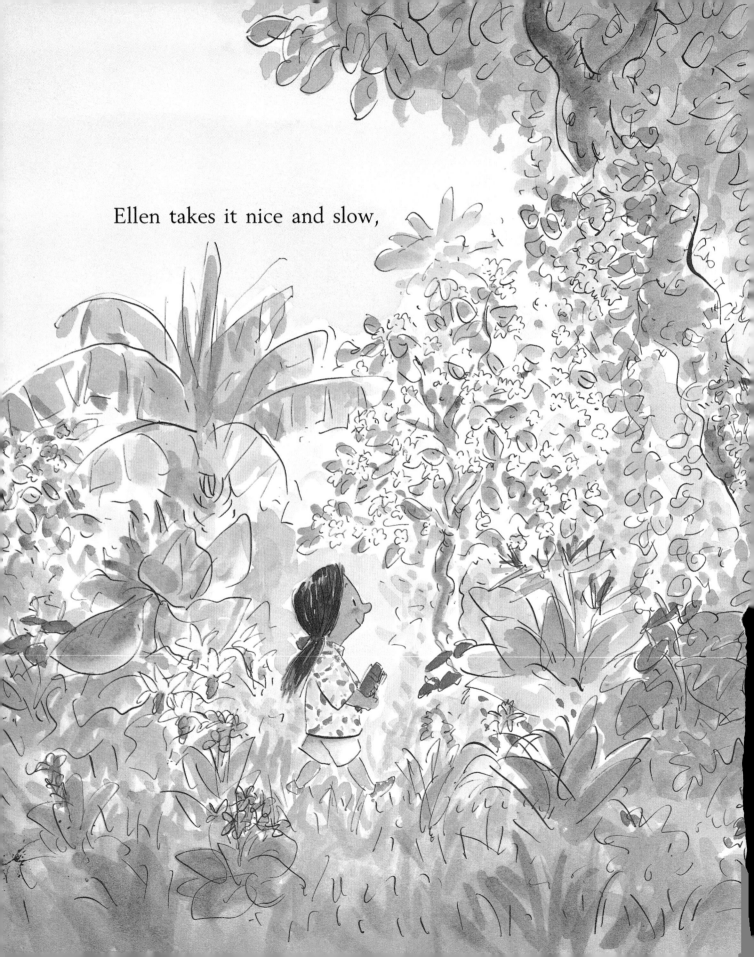

Ellen takes it nice and slow,

time to watch the flowers grow.

Liz and Larry, as a rule,
wear their jogging shoes to school.

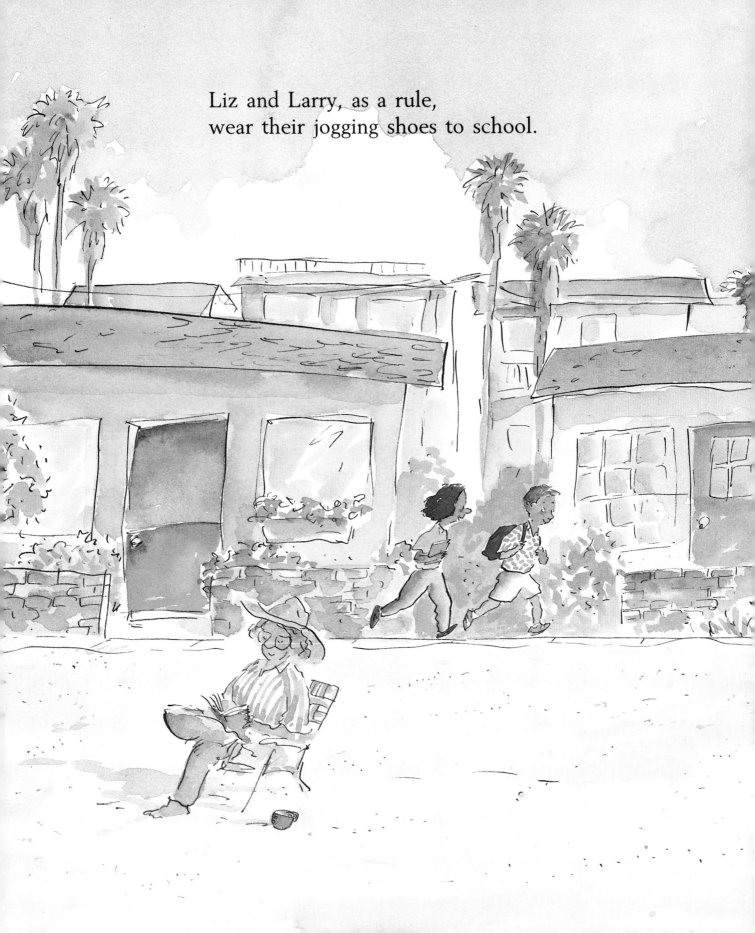

But at twenty minutes past,
roller skates are twice as fast.

And the fastest way by far

is by school bus or by car!

Jenny, Jerry, Pete, and Perry

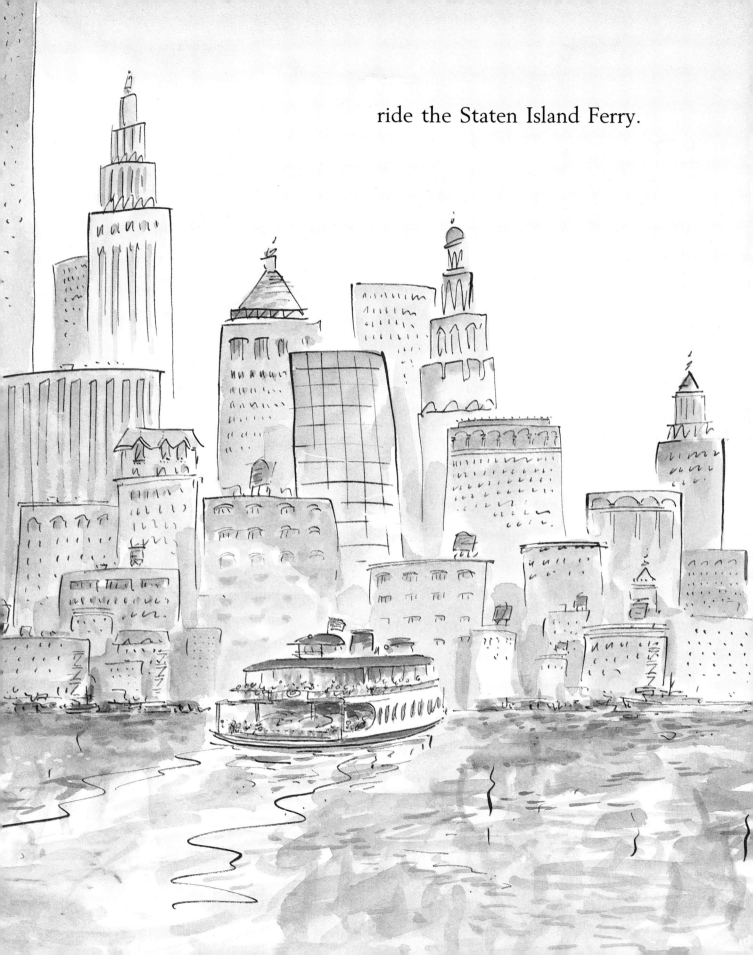

ride the Staten Island Ferry.

Cable cars take Jack and Jill
up the hill —

and down the hill.

Michael and his friend Miguel
see the rooftops from the El.

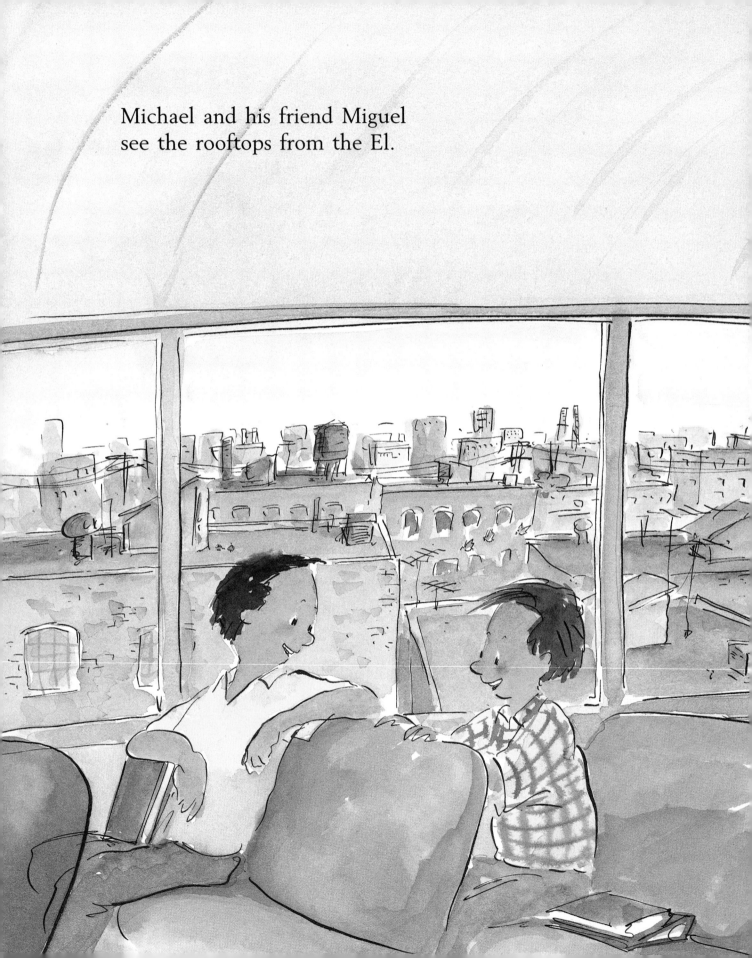

Horse-and-buggy rides, it's plain,
start the day for Jake and Jane.

And in Philly, Mitch and Molly
go to school by trackless trolley!

Bianca, Beppo, Benedetto
ride aboard the *vaporetto*.

Bundled up against the breeze,

Niels and Solveig go on skis.

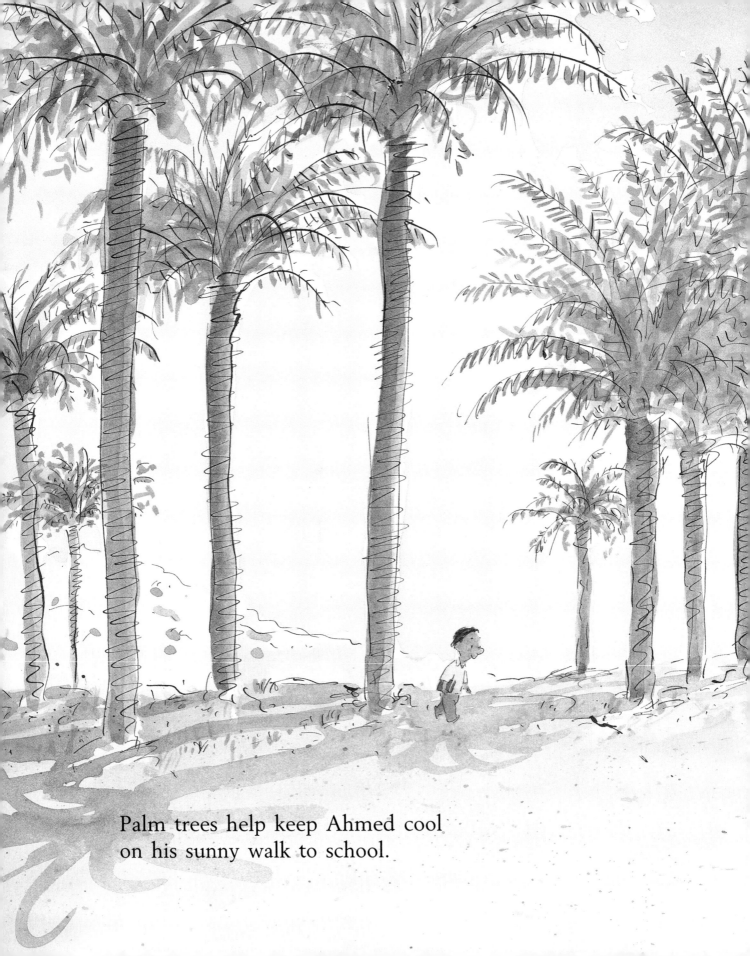

Palm trees help keep Ahmed cool
on his sunny walk to school.

Mira takes time out to play,
school's a hop and skip away.

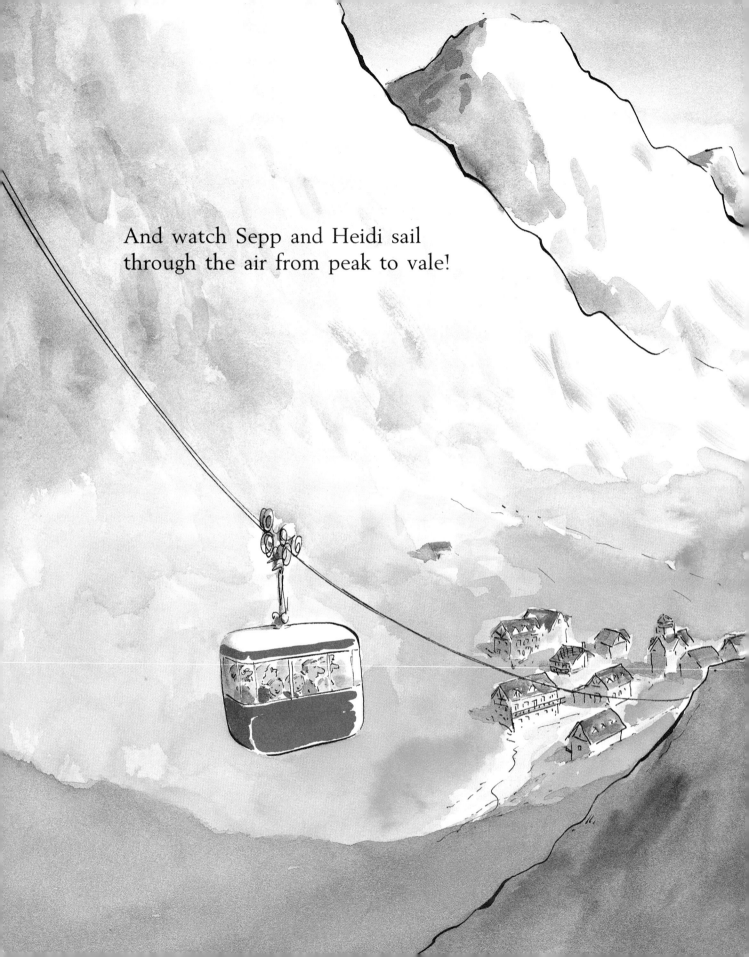

And watch Sepp and Heidi sail
through the air from peak to vale!

Akinyi leaves for school by train,
far across the mountain chain.

Kay and Fay and Flo and Joe
go to school by radio.

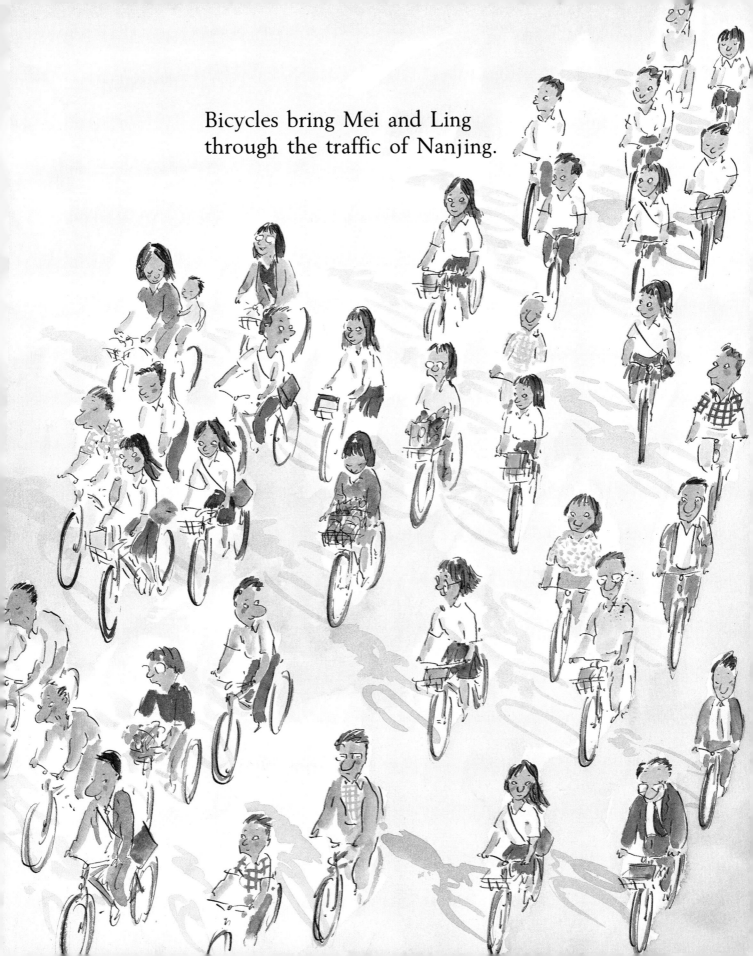

Bicycles bring Mei and Ling
through the traffic of Nanjing.

And beneath the dripping sky,
Ram is riding high and dry.

William comes ashore by boat,
counting sea gulls while afloat.

Carlos takes the town in stride.

Luz prefers the countryside.

And the famous Metro line
suits Igor and Ilyana fine.

Go by Copter?

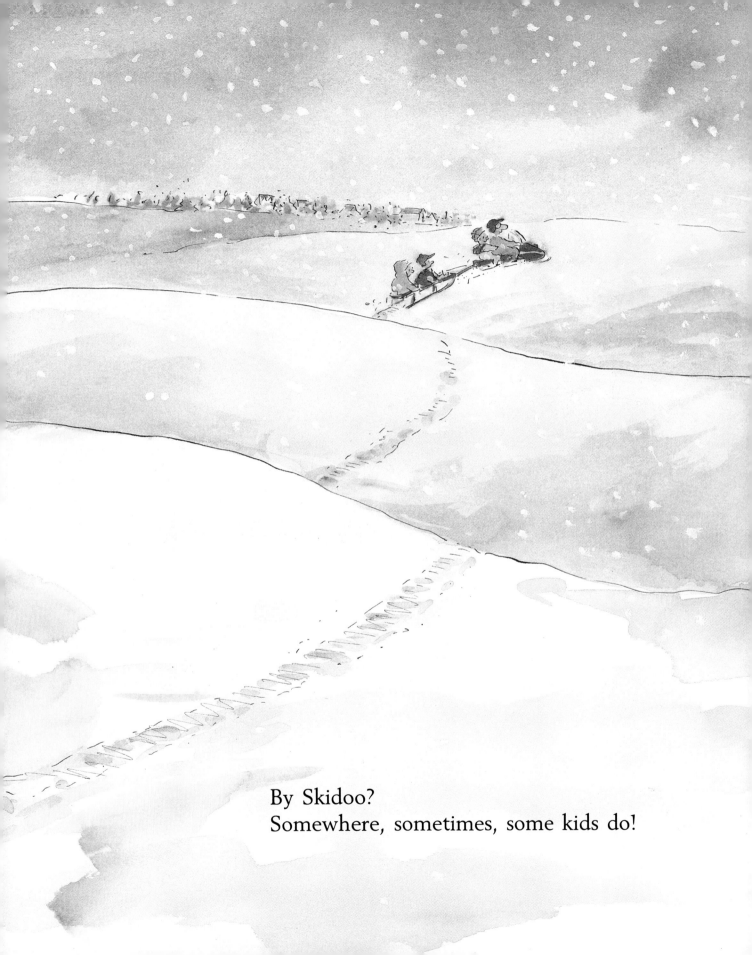

By Skidoo?
Somewhere, sometimes, some kids do!

You come, too! We'll look for you.

THIS IS WHERE WE LIVE

Ellen lives in Hawaii, U.S.A.
Liz and Larry and the skater live in California, U.S.A.
The bus and car riders live in Raytown, Missouri, U.S.A.
Jenny, Jerry, Pete, and Perry live in Staten Island, New York, U.S.A.
Jack and Jill live in San Francisco, California, U.S.A.
Michael and Miguel live in Chicago, Illinois, U.S.A.
Jake and Jane live in Lancaster, Pennsylvania, U.S.A.
Mitch and Molly live in Philadelphia, Pennsylvania, U.S.A.
Bianca, Beppo, and Benedetto live in Venice, Italy.
Niels and Solveig live in Norway.
Ahmed lives in Egypt.
Mira lives in Israel.
Sepp and Heidi live in Switzerland.
Akinyi lives in Kenya.
Kay, Fay, Flo, and Joe live in Australia.
Mei and Ling live in China.
Ram lives in India.
William lives in Maine, U.S.A.
Carlos and Luz live in Mexico.
Igor and Ilyana live in Moscow, U.S.S.R.
The Copter passengers live in Siberia, U.S.S.R.
The Skidoo passengers live in Canada.

① Ellen	⑦ Jake and Jane
② Liz and Larry and the skater	⑧ Mitch and Molly
③ The bus and car riders	⑨ Bianca, Beppo, and Benedetto
④ Jenny, Jerry, Pete, and Perry	⑩ Niels and Solveig
⑤ Jack and Jill	⑪ Ahmed
⑥ Michael and Miguel	⑫ Mira

⑬ Sepp and Heidi
⑭ Akinyi
⑮ Kay, Fay, Flo, and Joe
⑯ Mei and Ling
⑰ Ram
⑱ William

⑲ Carlos
⑳ Luz
㉑ Igor and Ilyana
㉒ The Copter passengers
㉓ The Skidoo passengers